Helping Children See Jesus

ISBN: 978-1-64104-042-6

FAITH
Taking God at His Word
New Testament Volume 5: Life of Christ Part 5

Author: Ruth B. Greiner
Illustrator: Frances H. Hertzler
Computer Graphic Artist: Ed Olson
Typesetting and Layout: Patricia Pope

© 2018 Bible Visuals International
PO Box 153, Akron, PA 17501-0153
Phone: (717) 859-1131
www.biblevisuals.org

All rights reserved. No part of this publication may be reproduced, stored in a retrieval system or transmitted in any form by any means, electronic, mechanical, photocopy, recording or otherwise, without the prior permission of the publisher, except as provided by USA copyright law.

RELATED ITEMS

To access related items (such as activities, memory verse posters and translated texts) please visit our web store at www.biblevisuals.org and enter 1005 at the top right of the web page. You may need to reduce the zoom setting to get the search box.

FREE TEXT DOWNLOAD

To obtain a FREE printable copy of the English teaching text (PDF format) under Product Format, please scroll down and select Extra–PDF Teacher Text Download. Then under Language select English before clicking the ADD TO CART button to place in your shopping cart. Other languages are available at an additional cost from the Language menu. When checking out, use coupon code XTACSV17 at checkout and click on Apply Coupon to receive the discount on the English text.

For by grace are ye saved through faith; and that not of yourselves; it is the gift of God: Not of works, lest any man should boast. Ephesians 2:8, 9

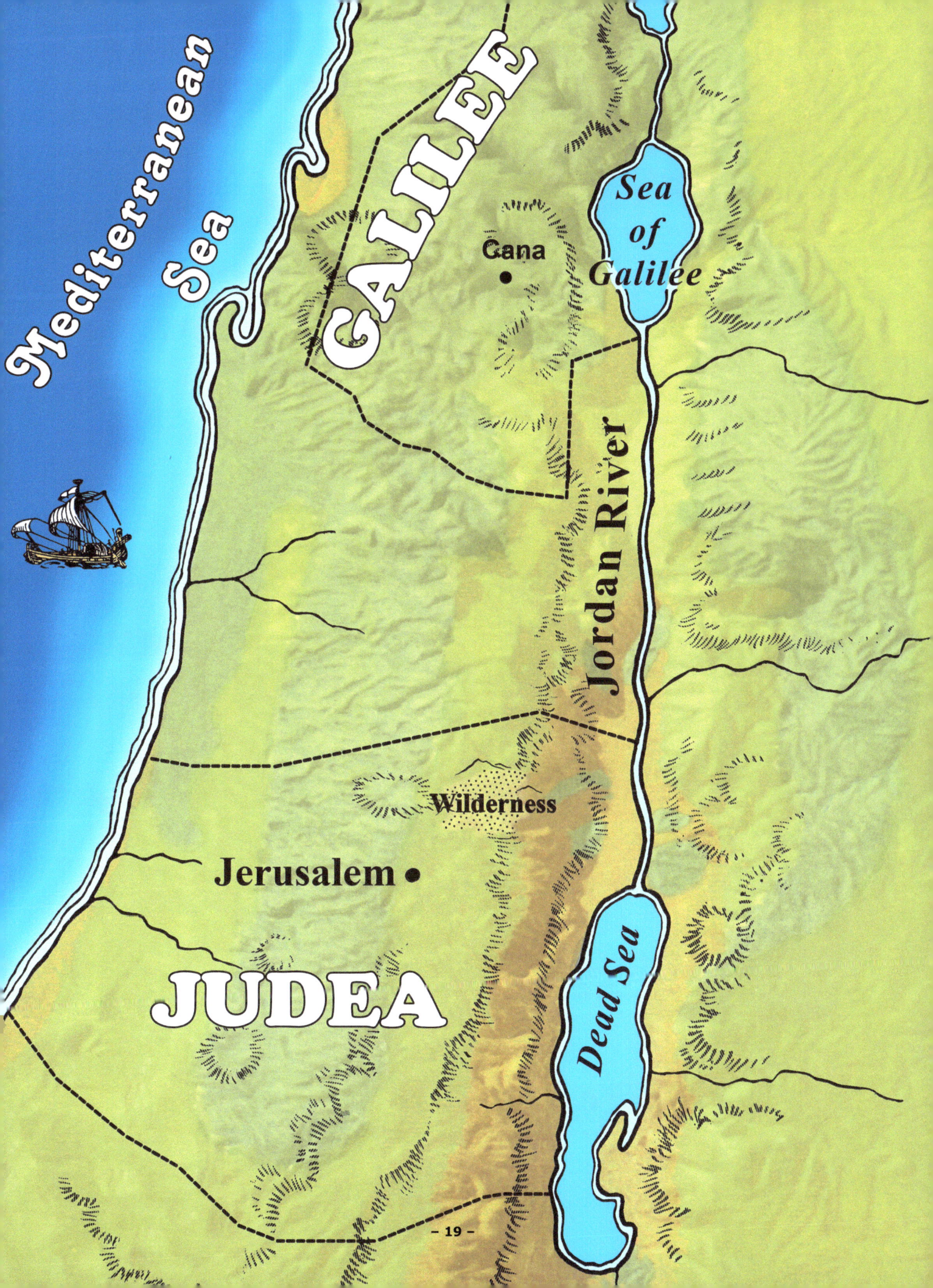

Lesson 1
HEALING OF THE NOBLEMAN'S SON

Scripture to be studied: John 4:46-54

The *aim* of the lesson: To teach your students that faith is (1) believing in the Lord Jesus Christ and taking Him at His word, (2) believing without seeing, (3) involves obedience.

What your students should *know*: God and His precious Son are completely trustworthy.

What your students should *feel*: An earnest desire to put their trust in the Lord Jesus Christ.

What your students should *do*: Believe in the Lord Jesus Christ as the Son of God and receive Him as Saviour.

Lesson outline (for the teacher's and students' notebooks):
1. The nobleman decides to ask Jesus for help (John 4:46).
2. The nobleman goes to Jesus (John 4:47).
3. The nobleman believes what Jesus says (John 4:47-50).
4. The servants report the son is healed (John 4:51-54).
5. The man sees his son is healed.

The verses to be memorized:

For by grace are ye saved through faith; and that not of yourselves, it is the gift of God: Not of works, lest any man should boast. (Ephesians 2:8-9)

> **NOTE TO THE TEACHER**
> Please study carefully the teacher's material which appears on page 2.

THE LESSON

Our memory verses say we are "saved through faith"– faith which is "the gift of God." Let us think for a moment of the word *faith*. Exactly what does it mean? (Teacher: Have a discussion.) Suppose you wanted to explain *faith* to someone else; what object could you use to help another know the meaning of *faith*? (Give students time to think about this and listen to their suggestions.)

Now let me tell you how a Bible teacher explains the meaning of faith. "I'm quite tired and want to sit down on this chair and rest. (You may use "bench" or "log" or whatever you use in your classroom.) But I don't know whether or not I can trust this chair. It looks like a good chair. It appears to be solid. I think it would hold me. But I'm still a bit doubtful. Have any of you sat on this chair? Did it hold you? It did? But I still wonder if it will hold me . . . I'll never get any rest from this chair until I'am willing to trust it and sit down. (Do so now.)

From *Easy Object Lessons*. Published by Moody Press, Chicago, IL, 60610. Copyright 1970. Used by permission.

If you want rest from sin, you must be willing to trust the Lord Jesus Christ. Trusting Him means to have faith in Him.[1]

Listen carefully so you will learn from the Word of God how one man used faith. Then, at the close of the lesson, you can write in your notebook the truths you have learned about faith.

1. THE NOBLEMAN DECIDES TO ASK JESUS FOR HELP
John 4:46

Show Illustration #1

In the city of Capernaum lived a nobleman, an officer of the king. This nobleman had plenty of money, a fine home and servants. He also had a son whom he loved very much. He took special care of his son, hoping he, too, would some day become an officer of the king.

But something happened which caused the nobleman great sadness. His son became sick, tossing with a high fever. The boy would die unless somewhere a cure could be found. But where? Who was wise enough to know how to control the fever? Not one in Capernaum could make the sick boy well.

2. THE NOBLEMAN GOES TO JESUS
John 4:47

When all hope seemed gone, the father decided to go to the great Miracle Worker, the Lord Jesus Christ. The man had no understanding of the true nature of the Lord Jesus. He had not been taught (as you have) that Jesus is the Son of God. But he did feel that Jesus was One who could help. He had doubtless heard that, at a wedding in his own province of Galilee, the Lord Jesus turned water to wine. *If the Lord Jesus can do such a miracle,* the nobleman reasoned, *He can surely heal my son.*

Now Jesus was in Cana–about 25 miles (40 kilometers) away from the Capernaum home of the nobleman. That is a long distance. (Teacher: Mention some village which is 25 miles from your own so your students will have an idea as to the distance between Capernaum and Cana.)

Show Illustration #2

It probably took the man most of two days to walk to Cana. As he went, he wondered: *Will Jesus still be in Cana when I get there? Will He take time to listen to me? Will He really be able to make my son well? If only I could get there faster! Will I be too late?*

3. THE NOBLEMAN BELIEVES WHAT JESUS SAYS
John 4:47-50

Show Illustration #3

At last he arrived in Cana. When he found Jesus, the nobleman begged: "Please come to Capernaum and heal my son. He is about to die." Imagine that! He wanted the Lord Jesus to go 25 long miles to do something for his son.

The man was surprised when the Lord Jesus answered, "You will not believe in Me unless you see a miracle."

The Lord Jesus wants to be trusted. He wanted the man to believe that He is the Son of God. To have faith in the Lord Jesus as Saviour is the most important thing in life. It is far more important than to be healed.

The poor father was so fearful of losing his son that he did not seem to understand what the Lord Jesus meant. So he exclaimed, "Come, before my child dies!" The nobleman believed the Miracle Worker, Jesus, could do something if he could get Him to his son.

NOTE TO THE TEACHER

Before you can teach any doctrinal truth, you must clearly understand that doctrine. Therefore, before teaching these lessons, please make a Biblical study of faith. We all use ordinary faith every day: we walk across a bridge because we believe it will hold us; we accept a glass of water and drink it because we believe it is water. All faith–even the ordinary kind we use each day–comes from God. He has made us in such a way that we have faith. When anyone has saving faith in the Lord Jesus, it is: (1) because of the work of God; and (2) because a person's entire personality is at work.

Here is an excellent outline for your teacher's notebook:

FAITH

Another word for faith is belief. The New Testament uses these two words about 150 times. Always the meaning is the same: a sinner is declared to be saved by believing–or by having *faith*.

God alone saves the soul.

God saves only through the sacrifice of His Son.

A person can be saved only by believing the message of God.

Believing is the opposite of doing.

Study these verses in the Gospel of John: 1:12; 3:16, 36; 5:24; 6:29; 20:31; also Acts 16:31; Romans 1:16; 3:22; 4:5, 24; 5:1; 10:4; Galatians 3:22.

I. In the exercise of true faith, the whole personality is involved:
   A. *Knowledge* is necessary. (See Romans 10:13-17.)
      1. We must know *what* and *whom* to believe.
      2. Faith rests upon the Word of God.
      Knowledge alone, however, is not enough. So:
   B. *Assent* is necessary. (See Matthew 9:28.)
      We must give assent to our knowledge. Having *knowledge* of certain truths, and giving *assent* of the mind to those truths is not enough. So:
   C. *Appropriation* is necessary. (See John 1:12.)
      I myself must take possession of the things which I know, believing them for myself.
II. True Biblical faith is used in connection with:
   A. *God* (Study Hebrews 11:6; Acts 27:22-25; Romans 4:19-21; Genesis 15:4-6.)
      1. We must have absolute faith in the existence of God.
      2. Faith believes all God says is absolutely true.
   B. *The Lord Jesus Christ*
      1. There must be a *knowledge* of His claims. (Study John 9:35-38; John 10:30; Philippians 2:6-11.)
      2. There must be an *assent* to His claims. (Study John 16:30; 20:28; Matthew 16:16; John 6:68-69.)
      After we have the knowledge that Jesus is able to save and that He is the Saviour of the world, we must give assent to our knowledge.
      3. There must be a personal *appropriation* of Christ. (See John 1:12.)
      We not only believe *about* Christ, we must turn ourselves over to Christ. (That is, surrendering to a Person, not to mere faith in a creed.)
   C. *Prayer* (See 1 John 5:14-15.)
      1. There must be k*nowledge* of the promises on which we base our prayers.
      2. We must believe (*assenting* in the mind) that the promises are for us. (See Romans 4:20.)
      3. We must *appropriate* the promises. (See James 1:5-7.)
      Real faith thanks God for the thing asked for (if it is in accord with the will of God), even before receiving it. (See Mark 11:24.)
III. The Source of Faith
   Where does faith come from?
   A. It is from God.
      1. God the Father (See Romans 12:3.)
      2. God the Son (See Hebrews 12:2.)
      3. God the Spirit (See Galatians 5:22.)
   B. There is a human side of faith. (See Romans 10:17.)
      Faith is produced by having a knowledge of the Word of God and the God of the Word.
      Our faith grows by using the faith we already have. (See Luke 17:5-6.)
      We not only believe about Christ, we must turn ourselves over to Christ. (That is, surrendering to a Person, not to mere faith in a creed.)
   C. Prayer. (See 1 John 5:14-15.)
      1. There must be knowledge of the promises on which we base our prayers.
      2. We must believe (assenting in the mind) that the promises are for us. (See Romans 4:20.)
      3. We must appropriate the promises. (See James 1:5-7.)
      Real faith thanks God for the thing asked for (if it is in accord with the will of God), even before receiving it. (See Mark 11:24.)
IV. The Results of Faith
   A. We are saved by faith. (Study John 1:12; Romans 5:1; Galatians 3:26; Acts 26:18; 1 Peter 1:5.)
   B. We have rest, peace, assurance and joy. (See Isaiah 26:3; Romans 5:1; John 14:1; 1 Peter 1:8.)
   Now study carefully the text for the first lesson on *faith*: John 4:46-54.

In Lesson #1 you will introduce the subject of *faith*, explaining that:

1. Faith is believing in the Lord Jesus Christ and taking Him at His word.
2. Faith is believing without seeing.
3. Faith involves obedience.

God, His Son and His Word are completely trustworthy.

The Lord Jesus looked with pity on the man. "You may go home," He said. "Your son is alive and well."

Alive and well! The nobleman could scarcely believe it. How could it be true? How could Jesus have healed his son far away? But the nobleman did not question Jesus. The Lord had said his son was alive and well. And the nobleman believed Him. First, he believed Jesus could heal the boy if Jesus could get to him. Then he believed Jesus could make him well even though the boy was far away.

4. THE SERVANTS REPORT THE SON IS HEALED
John 4:51-54

Happily the nobleman started home. One mile, two, then three. On and on he went the rest of the day. The next morning he hurried faster than ever.

Show Illustration #4

As he neared Capernaum, he saw his servants rushing to him. "Your son is alive and well!" they shouted.

"When did it happen? When did he start to get better?" the nobleman demanded.

"Yesterday afternoon at one o'clock his fever left him."

The nobleman exclaimed, "That is exactly the hour when Jesus said, 'You may go home. Your son is alive and well!'"

5. THE MAN SEES HIS SON IS HEALED

Show Illustration #5

He rushed to his home and saw his son completely well again. Do you think the man told the boy and his family and the servants what had happened? Indeed he did! He told them about the Miracle Worker Jesus. He told them all that the Lord Jesus and he had said to each other. He could have explained:

First: I believed if Jesus could get here, He could heal my son.

Second: I believed *the word of Jesus* when He told me my son was well.

Third: Now I believe *in Jesus*. I believe He is the Son of God. I receive Him as my own Saviour.

The people in his house listened to all the nobleman said. And then–right then–everyone in the house did the most important thing in life: they believed in Jesus, the Son of God. They had faith. Do *you* believe in Him?

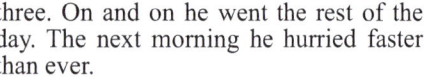

Lesson 2
THE DAUGHTER OF JAIRUS

NOTE TO THE TEACHER

Your students may question why the woman touched the robe of the Lord Jesus secretly. Here is the answer:

"We can understand what was behind this woman's secrecy. A perfectly natural modesty and embarrassment because of the nature of her disease, the shame of her brazenness and the unlawfulness of her appearance in public, caused her to shrink from approaching the Lord openly.

"According to the Levitical code a woman suffering as she had been suffering was considered unclean. The one she touched was also decreed ceremonially unclean until the evening (Leviticus 15:25-27). No wonder this woman hoped to act unnoticed by the Lord Jesus. But He looked beyond the immediate circumstances. We can be sure that He took no pleasure in embarrassing her, but He honored her faith. And He longed that she should have the joy of assured salvation, and that all should witness His power.

"Thus it was that He sought her out from the crowd, and that when she, 'fearing and trembling. . . fell down before Him, and told Him the truth,' He blessed her: 'Daughter (indicating a new relationship), your faith has made you whole; go in (literally, into) peace, and be whole of your plague.' What a difference this made to the woman! No longer did she need to hide her blessing. Not only had the healing of her body been effected, but her soul had been cleansed also. She had entered into a personal relationship with the Lord. She had fallen down before Him with a troubled soul; she departed 'into peace.'

"The shame of the moment was worthwhile now. The suffering of the years had been nullified through the cleansing, healing, saving power of the Son of God. And in her confession before Him she had borne witness to His person and to His work. Her faith had saved her. But her faith was not the power of her release–it was the channel through which the power of the Lord Jesus Christ was able to operate. No matter how great the faith, unless it is centered in Him who has the power to save and to bless, it is valueless."

From *Studies in the Gospel According to Mark* by E. Schuyler English. Used by permission.

Scripture to be studied: Matthew 9:18-26; Mark 5:21-43; Luke 8:40-56

The *aim* of the lesson: To teach your students how faith works.

What your students should *know*: All faith comes from God.

What your students should *feel*: Challenged to trust God completely.

What your students should *do*: Believe that Jesus is the Son of God and place their full trust in Him.

Lesson outline (for the teacher's and students' notebooks):

1. A father believes Jesus can heal his daughter (Matthew 9:18-19; Mark 5:21-24; Luke 8:40-42).
2. A woman believes she can be healed (Matthew 9:20-22; Mark 5:25-32; Luke 8:43-46).
3. The woman's faith is rewarded (Matthew 9:22; Mark 5:33-34; Luke 8:47-48).
4. Jesus tells the sad father to believe (Matthew 9:23-24; Mark 5:35-40; Luke 8:49-53).
5. Because the father believes Jesus, Jesus does a miracle (Matthew 9:25-26; Mark 5:40-43; Luke 8:54-56).

The verses to be memorized:

For by grace are ye saved through faith; and that not of yourselves, it is the gift of God: Not of works, lest any man should boast. (Ephesians 2:8-9)

THE LESSON

In our last study we learned what faith is. Who will tell me what it is? (Give students opportunity to explain.) Who used faith in that lesson and how do we know he had faith? (Again, let students discuss.) Today we shall learn how two others used their faith. Listen carefully!

1. A FATHER BELIEVES JESUS CAN HEAL HIS DAUGHTER
Matthew 9:18-19; Mark 5:21-24; Luke 8:40-42

By the Sea of Galilee, not far from the city of Capernaum, great crowds of people stood waiting. They wanted to see Jesus who was crossing the lake in a boat.

When the boat touched shore, Jesus and His disciples stepped out. Gladly the people welcomed Him and listened as He talked to them. One man, named Jairus, was an important leader in the Jewish synagogue. (The synagogue was the place where the Jews worshiped God.) Most of the leaders in the synagogue, however, did not believe in Jesus as the Son of God.

Show Illustration #6

Jairus pushed his way through the crowd and fell at the feet of Jesus. Looking up into the most wonderful face he had ever seen, Jairus sobbed, "My little girl is dying! Please come and place Your hands on her so she will get well and live."

Had he heard that the Lord Jesus healed the son of the nobleman? Perhaps so. Few Jews, however, believed that the Lord Jesus was the Son of God. (See John 1:11.) But Jairus was desperate. He had to have someone who could heal his only daughter.

When the crowd saw the Lord Jesus turn to follow Jairus, they determined to go with Him. Perhaps they would see Him do a miracle for Jairus. They had heard of the wonderful things Jesus did for others. Now they wanted to see a miracle with their own eyes. The crowds pushed and pressed against Jesus. Everyone wanted to be near Him. Jairus thought Jesus would never get to his little girl.

2. A WOMAN BELIEVES SHE CAN BE HEALED
Matthew 9:20-22; Mark 5:25-32; Luke 8:43-46

Show Illustration #7

Right then Jesus asked, "Who touched Me?"

"Not I." "Nor did I," another answered.

Peter and the other disciples of Jesus said, "Lord, a great crowd has been thronging You all day long. Many people have touched You. How can you ask, 'Who touched Me?'"

Turning about, Jesus looked into the face of the woman who had touched Him. There are no secrets with Him. He knew who had touched Him. But how did He know her touch was different from the rest who pushed in on Him? Because He who knows all things, knew that only one had a particular need and touched Him for a purpose.

3. THE WOMAN'S FAITH IS REWARDED
Matthew 9:22; Mark 5:33-34; Luke 8:47-48

Show Illustration #8

The woman trembled as she fell at the feet of Jesus. "I have been sick for twelve years with a bleeding that would not stop," she said. "I have been to many doctors and spent all my money. But instead of getting better, I have become worse. I heard that You heal sick people. I believed that if I could only touch Your clothes, I would be well. So I shoved through the crowd and touched the edge of Your robe."

The moment the woman touched Him, Jesus knew His power entered her body. He was not angry with her. Instead, because of her faith, He named her as His child, saying, "Daughter, all is well. Your faith has made you well. Go in peace and be healed."

What a happy day it was for that woman! Because she believed in the Lord Jesus, He gave her His peace. He cleansed her of her sin. She had fallen before Him afraid. She went away in peace. Her faith in the Lord Jesus saved her. And she was well–completely well!

4. JESUS TELLS THE SAD FATHER TO BELIEVE
Matthew 9:23-24; Mark 5:35-40; Luke 8:49-53

Show Illustration #9

Jairus was impatient. Had the Lord Jesus forgotten Him? He pushed closer to remind Jesus of his sick daughter.

At that moment a messenger ran to Jairus. "Your daughter is dead," he said. "It is no use to bother the Master now."

Poor Jairus! He thought: *Why did that woman have to delay us? Why did the Lord Jesus stop to talk with her? She has been sick so long that she could have waited until after my child had been cared for. Now my only daughter is dead!*

But the Lord Jesus said, "Do not be afraid. Keep believing in Me and your daughter will be all right." This is not a time for fear, Jairus. This is a time for faith!

Jesus ordered the crowd to stop following Him. Taking only three of His disciples (Peter, James and John), He went with Jairus to his home.

Show Illustration #10

What crying was going on there! Family, friends and outsiders–whose business it was to cry when someone died–all were wailing loudly.

The Lord Jesus asked, "Why are you making such a noise? Why are you crying? The child is not dead. She is sleeping!"

Why did Jesus say that when all the people knew the girl was dead? He said it because He knows more than anyone else. He knows that for the Christian, death is like being asleep. (See John 11:11, 13,

26.) Because the people who were crying did not understand what Jesus knew, they laughed at Him.

5. BECAUSE THE FATHER BELIEVES JESUS, JESUS DOES A MIRACLE
Matthew 9:25-26; Mark 5:40-43; Luke 8:54-56

Jesus sent the people outside. Then with her parents and His three disciples, the Lord went into the room where the 12-year-old lay. She did not breathe. She did not, could not move.

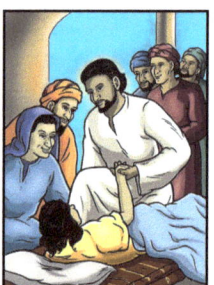

Show Illustration #11

Taking her by the hand, the Lord Jesus said gently, "Little girl, get up!"

Immediately the girl stood up and walked. She was alive. Her parents were astonished!

Jesus said, "Give her something to eat!" She did not need medicine. She was alive and completely well. Jesus, the Son of God, had done a miracle. His followers now understood He could do more than heal the sick. He had power also to raise the dead. Again He proved Himself to be the Son of God.

There are three ways in which Jairus and the sick woman were alike:

1. Both had *knowledge* about the Lord Jesus.
2. Both *believed in their minds* that He could help them.
3. Both of them *trusted Him with all their hearts*.

From whom did they receive their faith? From God. He gave each of them faith to believe.

For a sick person to be made well, or for a dead person to be brought back to life, is wonderful indeed. But to God, that which is most important is for all people everywhere to be saved. That is why He caused His precious Son, the Lord Jesus, to die on the cross for our sins.

Knowing about the Lord Jesus is not enough. *Thinking about* the Lord Jesus is not enough. *Believing He can do good things* is not enough.

We must believe that Jesus is the Son of God.
We must place our trust in Him, believing He died for our sin.
We must receive Him and turn from our sin.

Then, and only then, will we have His gift of salvation. (See Ephesians 2:8-9.)

Lesson 3
A BLIND MAN HEALED

NOTE TO THE TEACHER

"While every effort has been made to keep these lessons simple, it is not claimed that they are complete. The teacher is encouraged to take the seed thoughts contained in these pages, nurture them in his own heart and mind, and then present them to his class. In this way, under the guidance of the Holy Spirit, the lesson will become his own and the message will be the message of the Lord for that particular occasion. Even as canned food must be warmed and served attractively, so must prepared lesson material be warmed in the heart of the teacher and served to the class with careful preparation."

From *Easy-to-Give Object Lessons*. Published by Moody Press, Chicago, IL 60610. © 1974. Used by permission.

Scripture to be studied: John 9:1-38

The *aim* of the lesson: To teach your students the result of true faith.

What your students should *know*: The result of faith in Christ is forgiveness of sin and assurance of eternal life.

What your students should *feel*: A desire to be forgiven of sin and assured of eternal life.

What your students should *do*: Place their trust in the Lord Jesus Christ and receive forgiveness and assurance.

Lesson outline (for the teacher's and students' notebooks):

1. Blind–to show the power of God (John 9:1-5).
2. The blind man believes Jesus and obeys Him (John 9:6-7).
3. The blind man sees because he believed (John 9:7-13).
4. The Pharisees refuse to believe in Jesus (John 9:14-34).
5. The man places all His trust in Jesus (John 9:35-38).

The verses to be memorized:

For by grace are ye saved through faith; and that not of yourselves, it is the gift of God: Not of works, lest any man should boast. (Ephesians 2:8-9)

THE LESSON

What is faith? *Faith is believing God.* It is believing without seeing. How does a person have faith? The Bible tells us that "faith cometh by hearing, and hearing by the Word of God" (Romans 10:17). Today in our Bible lesson we shall learn the result of faith.

1. BLIND—TO SHOW THE POWER OF GOD
John 9:1-5

Show Illustration #12

It was the Sabbath day (Saturday), the Jewish day of worship. As Jesus and His disciples walked near the temple in Jerusalem, they met a blind beggar. The man had never seen the face of his mother or father. He had never seen the sun rise or set. Nor had he seen a bird fly. He had never seen his home. Because he was blind, he could not work as other men did. Instead he sat and begged for money and food.

Seeing him, the disciples turned to the Lord Jesus and whispered, "Why is this man blind? Is it because he sinned? Or is it because his parents sinned?" (We have learned, you remember, that sickness is *sometimes* the result of sin.)

"Neither his sin nor the sin of his parents caused his blindness. He was born blind to show the power of God," Jesus explained.

Every time they saw the Lord Jesus heal a person, the disciples saw the power of God. They looked at the blind man wondering, *Will we again see God's power?*

2. THE BLIND MAN BELIEVES JESUS AND OBEYS HIM
John 9:6-7

Show Illustration #13

Then the disciples saw Jesus spit on the ground and make clay. He spread the clay on the eyes of the blind man, saying, "Go and wash in the Pool of Siloam."

What a strange command! Could Jesus have healed the man without sending him to the pool? Yes. But He wanted the man to believe Him *and* obey Him. He wanted the man to use faith.

Obediently the blind beggar rose and felt his way to the Pool of Siloam. Reaching the pool, he bent low and washed.

3. THE BLIND MAN SEES BECAUSE HE BELIEVED
John 9:7-13

Show Illustration #14

As he lifted his head he blinked his eyes. The light startled him. He saw the pool with its shimmering water. He saw trees and flowers and buildings. He saw people. He saw colors: green grass, blue sky, red and yellow flowers. What a beautiful world!

He hurried home. *What will my parents say?* he wondered. *What will the neighbors say? What will the Jewish leaders say?*

Seeing him, the neighbors asked, "Is this the same man who used to sit and beg?"

"Yes," some said, "this is the man."

Others said, "No, it is someone who looks like him."

Then the man himself said, "I am the same man."

"How were your eyes opened?" they asked.

"A Man called Jesus made some clay and put it on my eyes. Then He told me to wash at the Pool of Siloam. So I went. And as soon as I washed, I could see!"

"Where is He?" the people demanded.

"I do not know," the man replied.

The people decided that the Pharisees should know about this. And they took the man to the Pharisees.

4. THE PHARISEES REFUSE TO BELIEVE IN JESUS
John 9:14-34

Show Illustration #15

When the Pharisees heard the news, they began to argue. Some said: "We have our laws that forbid us from doing such things as making clay and washing in a pool on the Sabbath. He did this miracle on the Sabbath, so we know He is not from God."

Others said, "But how could a man who is *not* from God do such mighty works?"

Turning again to the man, they asked, "This Man who opened your eyes . . . who is He?"

"He is a Prophet," he answered. His answer was right. Jesus is the Prophet sent from God. But He is more than a Prophet. He is the Son of God. However, the Pharisees did not believe this.

Turning to the parents of the man, they asked, "Is this your son? Was he born blind? How is it that now he can see?"

The parents were afraid to tell the truth. They knew if they said Jesus is the Christ (the Saviour, sent from God), they would be put out of the synagogue. Carefully the parents answered. "We know he is our son. He was born blind. But we do not know how he now can see. We do not know who opened his eyes. Ask him. He is old enough to answer for himself."

The Jewish leaders again called the man who had been blind. "Promise before God to tell the truth," they demanded. "We know this Man, Jesus, is a sinner."

"I do not know if He is a sinner or not," replied the man. "One thing I *do* know: I was blind. Now I see."

"What did He do to you?" they asked. "How did He open your eyes?"

"I already told you and you did not listen. Why do you want to hear it again? Maybe you would like to be His disciples?"

This made the Jewish leaders angry. They cursed him and said, "*You* are His disciple, but we are disciples of Moses. We know God has spoken to Moses. But as for that fellow (Jesus), we do not even know where He comes from." The Pharisees were supposed to know everything. But this was something they did not know.

The man answered: "What a strange thing! You do not know where He comes from, but He opened my eyes. We know God does not listen to sinners. But He does listen to those who worship Him–people who do what He wants them to do. Since the world began nobody ever heard of a man who was born blind being given his sight. If this Man had not been sent from God, He could have done nothing!"

The Pharisees had heard enough. They shouted angrily: "You who were born and raised in sin–are you trying to teach us?" And they threw him out of the synagogue so he could not worship God.

5. THE MAN PLACES ALL HIS TRUST IN JESUS
John 9:35-38

Show Illustration #16

When Jesus heard they had thrown him out, He found the man. He asked, "Do you believe in the Son of God?"

The man answered, "Tell me who He is, Sir, so I can believe in Him!"

Jesus said, "You have already seen Him, and He is the One who is talking with you now."

"Yes, Lord," the man said. "I do believe." Then he bowed low and worshiped Jesus.

Imagine that! After a lifetime of blind begging, the man said, "I believe." He saw the Lord Jesus face to face and worshiped Him! He was thrown from the synagogue into the loving arms of the Son of God.

What could be worse than being a blind beggar? This: Going through life without having faith in the Lord Jesus, the Son of God–not believing in Him as Saviour. Never having the assurance of forgiveness of sin. That is far, far worse than physical blindness.

You may do good deeds, thinking this may prepare you for Heaven. But God says there is only one way to be ready for Heaven: "For by grace are ye saved through faith; and that not of yourselves, it is the gift of God–not of works, lest any man should boast" (Ephesians 2:8-9).

What is faith? Faith is believing in God.

What does faith do? It causes me to understand that: Jesus Christ is the Son of God; He died on the cross in my place, taking the penalty for my sin; and that He rose again from the dead.

What is the result of faith? By putting all my trust in the Lord Jesus, the Saviour of the world, I have forgiveness of sin–and assurance of eternal life with Him in Heaven.

Do *you* have saving faith?

NOTE TO THE TEACHER

So that the subject of faith will become meaningful and practical to your class, review the teaching of the three previous lessons:

1. The meaning of faith
2. The working of faith
3. The results of faith

Ask God to help you make the doctrine of faith so simple that there will be the outworking of faith in the lives of your students.

Lesson 4
FAITH

The aim of the lesson: True faith includes believing in God, His Word and His Son.

What your students should *know*: The most important kind of faith is faith in God and His Son.

What your students should *feel*: A desire to believe on the Lord Jesus Christ.

What your students should *do*:
   Unsaved: Believe Jesus is the Son of God who took the punishment for their sins, and receive Him as their Saviour.
   Saved: Thank God for giving them saving faith.

Lesson outline (for the teacher's and students' notebooks):

1. Faith is believing without seeing (Hebrews 11:1).
2. Believing faith is rewarded (John 4:50-53; 9:1-7; Matthew 9:18-25).
3. Saving faith is believing that Jesus can forgive sin (Ephesians 2:8-9).

The verses to be memorized:

For by grace are ye saved through faith; and that not of yourselves, it is the gift of God: Not of works, lest any man should boast. (Ephesians 2:8-9)

THE LESSON

1. FAITH IS BELIEVING WITHOUT SEEING
Hebrews 11:1

(*Teacher:* Hold this book or your Bible high so all in the class can see it.)

Today I have a book in my hand. Am I telling the truth? How do you know I am telling the truth? (Allow time for response.) You know I am telling the truth because you can see I have a book in my hand. It is right here in view.

Now close your eyes and keep them closed until I tell you to open them. I do not want anyone to peek. (While their eyes are closed, put down your book and pick up a coin, small stone, or any object you can hide in a closed hand.)

Now while your eyes are closed I am going to tell you something. Are you ready? Keep your eyes closed! I am holding a coin in my hand. Do you believe I am telling the truth? Am I really holding a coin in my hand? (Give students an opportunity to answer. Some may answer "Yes," others "No.")

Some of you answered "Yes." What makes you say I have a coin in my hand? Can you see it with your eyes closed? Of course not. Now open your eyes. (Keep the coin hidden.) Can you see the coin? No. Do you still believe I am telling the truth? How many believe I have a coin in my hand? (Let them answer.) Some of you are not quite certain. Others really believe I do have a coin. You believe me even though you cannot see it. You have faith. Do you remember that word, *faith?* We talked about it in our past three lessons. *Faith* is an important word. It means *to believe even without seeing*. If you believe I have a coin in my hand even though you cannot see it, you have faith.

When I asked you a while ago if I had a book in my hand you said "Yes." Was that faith? No, because you could see the book. You believed because you saw. Faith, however, is believing even without seeing.

(Keep the coin hidden in your hand.)

Now I want someone who believes I have a coin in my hand to come get it. (Let one of the class take the coin from your hand.) You see, he came and took it. He did not see the coin, yet he believed I had it. And he believed I would give it to him. Was that faith? Yes it was.

It is important that we learn about faith–what it is and how it works. Do you know why? Because the Bible tells us that "without faith it is impossible to please" God (Hebrews 11:6). The most important kind of faith is faith in God–not faith in someone or something here on earth.

Faith means *to believe God* even though we have not seen Him. It means to believe in the Lord Jesus Christ, the Son of God, even though we have not seen Him. It means to believe that what God says is true.

How can we be certain God tells the truth? How do we know we can believe Him? Hebrews 6:18 says it is "impossible for God to lie," and Titus 1:2 says God "cannot lie." If God cannot lie, then He always tells the truth. Can we believe One who always tells the truth and never lies? Of course we can! The Lord Jesus, the Son of God, never lies because He is God the Son. (See John 10:30.) He can do nothing wrong. Everything that is said by God (Father and Son) is true. The Bible, the Word of God, is true. When you believe the Word of God (even if you may not understand it), you are exercising faith.

2. BELIEVING FAITH IS REWARDED
John 4:50-53; 9:1-7; Matthew 9:18-25

Can you think of some people in the Bible who had faith? (Give the class opportunity to mention several names.) You remember that a nobleman asked Jesus to heal his son. Did the nobleman have faith? Yes. Jesus said to him, "You may go home–your son is alive and well." The nobleman believed Jesus. God saw his faith and rewarded it.

Show Illustration #5

The nobleman went home and found his son well. Then the family of the nobleman believed, too. They all had faith in the Son of God, although they could not see Him.

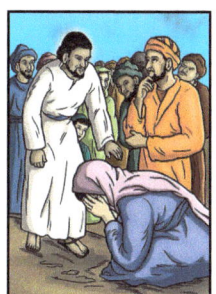

Show Illustration #8

The woman who was sick for twelve years trusted the Lord Jesus Christ. She believed He could make her well. So she simply reached out and touched the edge of His robe. The bleeding stopped immediately. Her faith was rewarded.

Jairus, too, had faith. He believed Jesus could make his daughter well. However, before Jesus could get to the girl, she died. But Jairus did not stop believing. Jesus helped him to keep on believing even when all hope seemed gone. God rewarded the faith of Jairus.

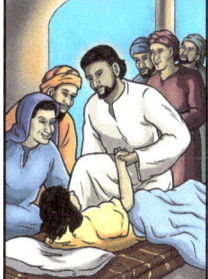

Show Illustration #11

His daughter was raised from the dead.

Show Illustration #14

Do you remember what happened to the blind man? The Lord Jesus put clay on his eyes and told him to wash at the Pool of Siloam. Did he obey? Yes, he did. He believed Jesus was telling the truth. He had faith in the Son of God and his eyes were opened.

3. BELIEVING JESUS CAN FORGIVE SIN IS SAVING FAITH
Ephesians 2:8-9

All these people believed the Lord Jesus could help them. They had faith in the power of God. They believed what He said. But more important than believing Jesus can make bodies well is believing He can forgive sin. This is called *saving faith*. It is the faith that makes you safe and ready for Heaven.

Do you believe the Lord Jesus Christ is the Son of God? Do you believe He died for your sins on the cross? Do you believe He rose from the dead? Have you received the Lord Jesus Christ as your Saviour? (See John 1:12.) If so, you have the faith that pleases God. He promises eternal life to all who have true faith in His Son, Jesus Christ.

Simply thinking about Jesus is not faith. Praying to God is not faith. Listening to people talk about God is not faith. Reading the Bible is not faith. It is good to do all these. But none of them can please God if you do not believe in Him.

When you (1) believe the Lord Jesus is the Son of God; (2) when you believe He took the punishment for your sin; (3) when you place your trust in Him as your Saviour–then God receives you into His family. The Lord Jesus takes your sin and you take God's righteousness. (See 2 Corinthians 5:21.) Eternal life and a home in Heaven can be yours because of the goodness and righteousness of God–not because of your good works. (See Titus 3:5.)

This doesn't mean we shouldn't do good deeds. When we receive the Lord Jesus Christ as Saviour, He comes to live in our hearts. Then we can and should please Him by doing good. Our lives are to be different. We receive a new life–the life of God. With this new life come many good things. Old things pass away and all things become new. (See 2 Corinthians 5:17; James 2:17.)

And God has rewards for men and women of faith. We cannot really know all that God has waiting for us until we get to Heaven.

(*Teacher:* hold up your Bible.)

This Book is the Word of God. We can see it. We can believe everything in this Book, because God cannot lie. This Book says: "For by grace are ye saved through faith; and that not of yourselves, it is the gift of God–not of works, lest any man should boast" (Ephesians 2:8-9).

Now will you close your eyes tightly, as you did at the beginning of our lesson? Can you see God? No, you cannot. Can you believe in Him? Yes! Can you believe everything He has said in His Word, the Bible? Yes! If you have never placed your trust in the Lord Jesus Christ, will you do so now, even though you cannot see Him? Will you receive Him as your own Saviour? If you have already received Him, will you thank the Lord Jesus for giving you saving faith?

www.ingramcontent.com/pod-product-compliance
Lightning Source LLC
Chambersburg PA
CBHW060807090426
42736CB00002B/185